THE SAPPHIRE AFFAIR

THE TRUE STORY BEHIND ALFED HITCHCOCK'S TOPAZ

STRANGER THAN FICTION SERIES #4

FERGUS MASON

Absolute Crime Press
ANAHEIM, CALIFORNIA

Contents

ABOUT ABSOLUTE CRIME

Absolute Crime publishes only the best true crime literature. Our focus is on the crimes that you've probably never heard of, but you are fascinated to read more about. With each engaging and gripping story, we try to let readers relive moments in history that some people have tried to forget.

Remember, our books are not meant for the faint at heart. We don't hold back--if a crime is bloody, we let the words splatter across the page so you can experience the crime in the most horrifying way!

If you enjoy this book, please visit our homepage (www.AbsoluteCrime.com) to see other books we offer; if you have any feedback, we'd love to hear from you!

Sign up for our mailing list, and we'll send you out a free true crime book!

http://www.absolutecrime.com/newsletter

INTRODUCTION

Sir Alfred Hitchcock was probably the best known movie director of the 20th century. Born in England in 1899, he directed his first film in Germany in 1922 and moved to Hollywood in 1939. By the late 1950s he was at the peak of the profession and his 1960 Psycho is one of the most iconic movies of all time. During his long career he specialized in suspense stories – tightly plotted thrillers that at their best could generate an incredible level of tension. It's no surprise that during the Cold War he turned his talent for suspense to the genre of espionage. Another characteristic of Hitchcock's work was that much if it was based – sometimes loosely, sometimes much more accurately – on real events. His murder classic Rope was inspired by teenage murderers Leopold and Loeb while Frenzy was partly inspired by the London serial killer Jack the Stripper. For the second of his two spy dramas he took on novel based on an extraordinary story of defection, treason and betrayal that had played out during one of the most dramatic events of the 1960s – the Cuban missile crisis.

When the Cold War ended in 1990 the atmosphere of terror that it inspired dissipated with remarkable speed. The 21st century has its own worries, including environmental catastrophe, climate change, globalization, poverty and international terrorism, and most people worry about at least some of these to some degree. None of them match the threat of nuclear war that hung over the world from the 1950s to the fall of the Berlin Wall. With tens of thousands of nuclear weapons on a hair trigger a single mistake could have demolished most of what human civilization has built in the last 5,000 years. If scientists like Carl Sagan were right, and a major strategic exchange would cause a nuclear winter, the planet could have been wiped clean of all life more complex than a cockroach. Not since the last ice age had there been such an overwhelming danger to the human race. In October 1962 it looked to millions of people like the politicians of both superpowers were determined to push the other across the fatal line of launching a nuclear strike. The fate of the world hung on Cuba, a troubled island state in the Caribbean.

Woven through the dramatic events in and around Cuba was a quieter but perhaps equally dangerous scandal – an enormous, deeply embedded network of Soviet spies at the heart of the NATO alliance. A senior KGB defector had revealed that his agency had penetrated the highest levels of the French government, military and intelligence services – but when a French agent tried to act he found himself blocked at every turn by his own superiors.

Pieced together by bestselling author Leon Uris, a personal friend of the man at the center of the spy scandal, the novel Topaz told the story of how the KGB had spread its influence so deeply into a major European nation that even when the plot was discovered it was impossible to do anything about it. Hitchcock was intrigued, and in 1969 he turned the story into a movie. Critics view Topaz as one of his less successful works but as a classic Cold War spy thriller it still has a lot to offer.

If you've seen Topaz and want to know more about the events that inspired it you could have a struggle on your hands. The missile crisis is well documented but the spy scandal – the Sapphire affair – has pretty much sunk into obscurity. There is information available if you know where to look for it though – some is buried in the dusty archives of intelligence agencies, but a lot of it can be found in equally dusty corners of the internet. If you have the time to hunt down and read grainy scans of old magazine articles and obscure books you could build up a good picture of what happened. If you don't have that much time, read on…

[1]

THE FRENCH CONNECTION

Almost every country has an external intelligence service, but the power and resources they have varies. Countries that follow an isolationist path don't tend to pay much attention to foreign intelligence gathering – until the Second World War the USA had no organized intelligence agencies at all, for example. European colonial powers, who needed to keep up to date on often rebellious foreign possessions, tended to take it a bit more seriously. Britain had set up the Secret Service Bureau in 1909 but had been running intelligence networks out of its embassies for centuries. Their traditional rival, France, also had a long history of spying; the Revolutionaries had a secret police force at home and sent intelligence collectors throughout Europe. Later, when France gained colonies around the world, they developed a global reach. France's military and intelligence services were practically wiped out by the German invasion in 1940, but when the Free French returned to France in 1944 they quickly established a new agency. Officially its purpose was to collect information to help with liberate Europe from Nazi rule; in practice it spent most of its time spying on French colonies as well as the British and American allies who were doing all the actual work of liberating France. The new service quickly became notorious for both its lack of scruples and its effectiveness. It was called the Service de Documentation Extérieure et de Contre-Espionnage (External Documentation and Counter-Espionage Service), which was quickly shortened to SDECE.

The SDECE was formed on April 19, 1944 by André Dewavrin, better known by his code-name "Colonel Passy." Dewavrin had escaped to Britain to join de Gaulle's Free French army and had become head of a special intelligence unit, the BCRA. This unit was mostly responsible for working with the French Resistance, and Dewavrin sometimes had to parachute into occupied France to meet with Resistance leaders. In late 1943 the BCRA was merged with the remains of the Deuxième Bureau, which had been the main French intelligence agency from 1871 until the German occupation, and the new organization was named DGSS. At first this was led by Deuxième Bureau chief Jacques Soustelle, but Dewavrin took command in October 1944 and became the first head of SDECE at the next reorganization.

The Resistance had been split into two factions; the Free French were aligned with the Gaullist faction, but there was also a strong communist Resistance movement. During the war the two cooperated most of the time but it was an uneasy alliance that sometimes broke down into open conflict. When the Allies invaded the Gaullists quickly began working to reduce communist power, and the SDECE was strongly anti-communist right from the start. After the Germans withdrew from France much of the agency's energy went to fighting against communist influence in the new government. They had many successes, but some covert communists slipped through the net. Some, it later emerged, had slipped into the SDECE itself.

In the early 1950s the SDECE began to turn its attention to the situation in Algeria. The North African nation had been colonized by the French in 1848 and was classed as a region of France itself. When decolonization gathered speed after the war many Algerians began demanding independence, which the French didn't want to give them. Violence broke out in 1954 and within a few years a full-scale civil war was raging between armed rebel groups, French settlers and the military. The SDECE, especially the notorious paramilitary Action Service, was dragged into the conflict. The counter-espionage side of the organization increasingly focused on hunting down insurgents and, after 1961, the anti-Gaullist Organisation Armée Secrète; looking for Soviet spies slipped steadily down their list of priorities, and the KGB wasn't slow to notice. They had a strong incentive to exploit the situation, too. As well as their constant effort to collect intelligence on western countries there was a chance to hammer a wedge into a crack in the NATO alliance.

The Atlantic Alliance

Europe in the late 1940s was a frightening place. The wartime alliance between the USSR and the west had rapidly fallen apart almost as soon as the fighting had stopped, and Europeans now watched nervously as the Soviet army imposed communism in the territory it had occupied. Europe wanted to start rebuilding after the war but it looked as if Stalin was determined to continue it. The Soviet military remained close to its wartime strength and stood ready to invade Western Europe at a moment's notice. Several European countries – the UK, France, the Netherlands, Belgium and Luxembourg – signed the Treaty of Brussels in 1948, promising to come to each other's defense in the event of a Soviet attack. That still wasn't enough of a security guarantee. US

President Harry S. Truman and British Prime Minister Clement Attlee were concerned that a hostile and aggressive USSR could expand even further into Europe unless the USA played an active part in defending the continent. The USA had its own worries about communist expansion in Asia and felt that a strong defense of Europe would prevent the Soviets from turning their full power east. They quickly went to work expanding the alliance.

NATO was formed with the signing of the North Atlantic Treaty on April 4, 1949. Its early members were the five Brussels Treaty states plus the USA, Canada, Iceland, Portugal, Italy, Norway and Denmark; Turkey and Greece joined in 1952 and West Germany in 1955. Together the European NATO members formed a continuous border with the Soviets and their satellite states; the Treaty meant that an attack on one member would be seen as an attack on them all, and the agreement was backed up by the USA's military force. With the bulk of the west's combat power now free to fight directly against any Soviet invasion, instead of being held back within its own countries, an aggressive move by the USSR suddenly became a much riskier business. The Soviets on the other hand were worried that the new alliance might invade them, and weakening it became a high priority.

France had been a founding member of NATO, but its relations with the other major powers were often difficult. Traditionally France had been the strongest land power in mainland Europe, balanced by British naval strength, but after two disastrous world wars its influence was greatly reduced. It was also politically unstable, and the civil war in Algeria combined with a dissatisfied army to create the real risk of a military coup. All that was changed in 1958 by one man.

When Germany invaded France in May 1940 Charles de Gaulle was a colonel commanding a tank regiment. Over the next month his unit – now expanded to a weak division - achieved one of the few French successes against the advancing Panzers, and as a reward he was promoted to brigadier general.1 He was also appointed as the cooperation officer with the British forces. When France surrendered he fled to Britain with a few other loyal officers and set himself up as the leader of the Free French. Winston Churchill admired de Gaulle – at first – and valued the loyalty he inspired among the Free French troops, so encouraged his activities.

The relationship wasn't an easy one though. De Gaulle had a huge ego which often irritated British, and later American, leaders. Once he told Churchill that the French people saw him as a reincarnation of Joan of Arc; Churchill replied that the English had had to burn the first one.2 Nevertheless Britain and the USA continued to support de Gaulle and arm the Free French, who took part in the liberation of France in 1944. De Gaulle immediately declared himself leader of the reestablished French Republic, and took over as prime minister. Already he resented the other Allied leaders, and tried to demand equal status with Churchill, Roosevelt and Stalin. He didn't get it, and his behavior was causing increasing anger. Although the Free French troops were equipped with American vehicles and weapons, and depended completely on resupply from US forces, de Gaulle began issuing them orders that conflicted with the Allied war plan. Fighting almost broke out when French troops refused to hand over the areas around Stuttgart and Karlsruhe to the US Army, because de Gaulle wanted to add western areas of Germany to France. Churchill, remembering how France's treatment of a defeated Germany in 1919 had led to the rise of Hitler, refused to allow this, and President Truman threatened to stop military supplies to the French if they didn't back down. When Germany surrendered on May 7, 1945 de Gaulle refused to allow any British troops to take part in the victory parade in Paris. Finally he sent Free French troops to occupy part of northern Italy; it was already occupied by American units, and the French threatened to attack them if they didn't withdraw. That was enough. Truman cut off all military supplies to France, earning the USA de Gaulle's lifelong dislike. Trouble continued in the Middle East, with the British being forced to step in when French troops began massacring pro-independence demonstrators in Syria. By this time Churchill was calling de Gaulle "one of the greatest dangers to European peace." The French forces in Syria refused to stop their attacks on the demonstrators – which by now included artillery and air bombardment – until the British moved up tanks and the request became an order. Relations between de Gaulle and the British never recovered.3

Although the Free French contribution to the war had been small and completely reliant on US and British support, de Gaulle resented not being given equal stature with the main Allied leaders. His ego was about to let him down badly though; many in France were fed up with his arrogant posturing, too.

The French Fourth Republic was established in November 1945, and on November 13 the assembly unanimously elected de Gaulle as head of state. He didn't like the constitution however, or the fact that the Communist Party had won the largest share of votes in the recent election. Now he demanded that the communists be barred from any important cabinet posts. Over the next two months the government blundered from crisis to crisis, with de

Gaulle repeatedly threatening to resign if his demands weren't met. Soon he was being accused of using his wartime record to blackmail the government. Finally, on January 20 1946, he resigned "in protest." He believed that the outraged French people would demand he was brought back with increased powers. They didn't; the war was over and the French were more interested in rebuilding than indulging in his whims. De Gaulle vanished into obscurity for the next 12 years and, under a Socialist president, France rebuilt its relationships with the allies de Gaulle detested and helped to found NATO.

Unfortunately France's chronic political instability didn't end with de Gaulle's resignation. The French defeat in Indochina didn't just lay the foundations for the Vietnam War; it also gave a boost to pro-independence campaigns in other French colonies. Morocco and Tunisia slipped away in the 1950s and Algeria was heading the same way. The French were determined to hold on to Algeria however, and the war quickly escalated out of control. The French settlers and their allies in the army were furious at what they saw as government weakness and France drifted towards a military coup. Many army officers were supporters of de Gaulle and in early 1958 the retired general's name began to appear again. Speeches, the media and announcements by army officers all suggested that what France needed was de Gaulle. On May 19 de Gaulle himself said that he was ready to take power if asked.

Now events spiraled rapidly towards a climax. On May 24 paratroopers from the army in Algeria took control of the Mediterranean island of Corsica. Hard-line Gaullist General Jacques Massu began planning for more paratroopers to seize airports throughout France with the aid of air force units, and an armored regiment based near Paris dusted off its tanks. Massu announced that unless de Gaulle was returned to power immediately the army would overthrow the government. Parliament had little choice and on May 29 the government resigned. De Gaulle took power and immediately dissolved the postwar Fourth Republic system. In its place he drew up the constitution for the Fifth Republic, which con-

centrated power in the hands of a strong pres-
idency. The first president of the Fifth Republic
was Charles de Gaulle.

The Politics of Grandeur

It didn't take long for de Gaulle to restart
his power games. First he betrayed the army
that had returned him to power by agreeing to
Algeria's independence; army officers and settlers formed the OAS and repeatedly tried to
kill him. Then he turned his attention to NATO.

The dominant members of NATO were the
USA and UK; one was a superpower and the
other still had the second most powerful navy
in the world, which was the key to keeping the
Atlantic trade routes open. They were also
NATO's two nuclear powers, meaning they
would be the ones to fight at the strategic level in the event of a war. While all NATO members had a political voice within the alliance
these two tended to dominate military mat-
ters. Now de Gaulle demanded equal status
for France. That might have been greeted with
tolerant amusement; his grandiose posturing

was well known. Less acceptable was his demand for an expansion of the mutual defense guarantee. The purpose of NATO was to resist Soviet expansion in Western Europe, so Article 5 – the clause in the treaty that established mutual defense – applied to any attack on a NATO member that occurred north of the Tropic of Cancer. De Gaulle insisted that NATO should also commit to defending France's colonial possessions. At the time France had just been defeated in a disastrous war in South East Asia and was embroiled in an equally disastrous one in Algeria; the other allies were utterly opposed to being dragged into the disintegration of the French empire. De Gaulle's demands were refused. In retaliation he withdrew the French Mediterranean fleet from NATO command and ordered the USA to remove all its nuclear weapons from France.

France had a powerful army and air force, and by 1960 had developed its own nuclear weapons; it wasn't a vital component of the NATO order of battle, but it was certainly a useful one. NATO's headquarters was already located in France and if it had to be moved that would disrupt the alliance for months, possibly years. In the event of a war the French channel ports would also be vital to NATO. If tension rose in Europe NATO planned to reinforce its front line armies with British Army units from the UK and US forces flown in to the network of USAF bases in England; the quickest way for these troops to get to mainland Europe was across the English Channel. The crossing from Dover to Calais takes only an hour and could be protected by an umbrella of surface to air missiles and fighter patrols; with the channel also protected by the Royal Navy the Soviets would have been unable to interfere with the operation. Take France out of the alliance, however, and things became very different. From Dover to Calais the sea journey is only 24 miles; the next closest port, Ostend in Belgium, is over 60 miles from the English coast, and the ports in Holland are even further away – over 150 miles in some cases. Soviet aircraft, missile boats and submarines operating out of the Baltic could take a heavy toll on the flow of reinforcements to Europe if the ships were forced to leave the Straits of

Dover and venture into the more open waters of the North Sea. Life would also be harder for NATO units once they were fighting on the battlefields of Germany because they would no longer have friendly space behind them to maneuver if necessary. With de Gaulle now openly trying to build a separate peace with the Soviets they faced the risk of being forced back and trapped against the French border. Further damaging relations between France and the rest of the alliance was a major goal for the Soviets, and by early 1962 it looked like they were pushing against an open door.

[2]

Fear In London

Hammersmith Bridge has been taking traffic across the Thames since 1887. The 700 foot long structure has survived two World Wars and three terrorist bombs, and now it's prized by architects as one of the country's finest Victorian iron bridges. It's also a popular place for rowers and boaters, including the London Corinthians Sailing Club. Corinthians members like to sail dinghies on the river, and some of them are dedicated enough to get out on the water in all sorts of weather. February 2, 1964 was dry and warm for that time of year – over 53°F – and some of the Corinthians took advantage of it to cruise down to Hammersmith. Near the bridge one of the crews had their outing abruptly ruined. Wedged against a floating pontoon moored to the bank was something that looked suspiciously like a body.

The sailors eased off the sheets, slowed and cautiously turned in to have a closer look. Sure enough, a bloated corpse was snagged against the pontoon.4 Spend any amount of time on the Thames in a small boat and you'll see all sorts of things floating by, but the nude body of a woman isn't one you're going to meet every day.

An autopsy found water in the dead woman's lungs, meaning she had probably died of drowning. That happens often enough – about 450 people a year accidentally drown in Britain – but the police were pretty sure this wasn't an accident. The woman had been stripped almost naked before she went in the water, leaving only a pair of stockings pulled down around her ankles. Some of her teeth had been knocked out and her stained underwear was crammed into her mouth. There were also marks that suggested she'd been at least partially strangled. The nudity and missing teeth hinted at a connection to Rees. When the body was identified as 30-year-old prostitute Hanna Tailford definite warning flags were raised.

Tailford had last been seen alive on January 24, and according to the pathologists the state of her body made it likely she'd been in the river for a week. That isn't actually a surprising length of time for a corpse to go undiscovered; the Thames in London is a busy river, but there's no shortage of places for a cadaver to float out of sight. Until tides or currents pull it out into the open there's no guarantee anybody will see it. Tailford could even have been under the pontoon since her death, just waiting for someone to sail close by in a low, open boat.

Like the first two victims Tailford had run away from home as a teenager, unable to settle in the northern mining town where she'd been brought up. In London she soon ended up on the streets. Selling herself hadn't always brought in enough money to live, and her long record of soliciting convictions was livened up by a few for theft. Once, pregnant, she even tried to sell the unborn child through a newspaper ad.5 There was more to her career than a desperate struggle for cash, though. Difficult as it was to get information from the other hookers, the Met Police slowly built up a picture of a life lived on the border between the sleaze of street vice and the big money of London's social scene. Tailford hadn't just been a prostitute, it turned out. She'd also been involved in the pornographic movie industry, and had been paid to entertain at society parties.

On April 8 Irene Lockwood, 26 years old, was found on a narrow mud beach only 300 yards upriver from where Tailford's corpse had been discovered. Lockwood had been alive the day before, loitering outside a pub in Chiswick. Now she'd been stripped, strangled – probably with her own underwear - and thrown in the river. The autopsy found that she'd been four months pregnant and inquiries among other girls soon revealed that she, like Rees, had been trying to get an abortion. This time there was no wondering if her death had been the result of an abortion gone wrong; Lockwood had clearly been murdered.

It wouldn't be hard to find someone who wanted Irene Lockwood dead. She was a notorious scam artist, who specialized in persuading clients to take their trousers off outside her bedroom so an accomplice could go through their pockets while she had sex with them. She'd also been involved in illegal late night card games that had left a lot of gamblers with a nasty feeling that they'd been cheated. (which they had.) There was a long list of people who hated her and her death, normally, wouldn't have been seen as all that surprising. In fact a friend of hers had been beaten to death in 1963 by a client she'd tried to blackmail with explicit photographs. Boosting your income through theft and blackmail depends on a steady supply of victims who're more frightened of embarrassment than they are of getting their hands dirty, and a misjudgment can be dangerous.

The police were spotting some disturbing similarities to the previous killings, though. Like Figg, Rees and Tailford, Lockwood was short – only five feet two. Rees and Tailford had also been pregnant and all four women had dark hair. (although Lockwood's was dyed blonde.) All four had suffered from sexually transmitted diseases during their careers in the sex trade. Three of them had been found along the same stretch of river in the space of five months. This was enough to make the cluster of killings stand out from the routine attrition of London's streetwalkers. It looked increasingly as if a serial killer was stalking hookers along the Thames in west London.

Once Lockwood was identified the police began taking her life apart searching for clues. Her diary referred to a man called "Kenny," and that looked like it might be a lead. Lockwood's gambling scam had been set up by Kenneth Archibald, the caretaker at Holland Park Tennis Club. Tennis clubs have an image as respectable organizations, and this one was – during the day. At night it was a bit different. At the time Britain had some of the strictest drinking laws in Europe and an evening out would be ended by the familiar 10:45pm call of "last orders please." That didn't suit everyone so in large cities there were always illegal drinking dens if you looked hard enough. These were often in private homes or lock-up garages, but Archibald went one better than that. His job put him in charge of a clubhouse with a fully equipped bar, and as long as it was in good shape during official opening hours there was nothing to stop him exploiting it. Operating by word of mouth Archibald turned the club into an illicit party venue, and it attracted a collection of shady characters. Late-night drinkers mingled with prostitutes and thrill seekers, and the club grounds and tennis courts provided plenty of secluded corners for sex. Lockwood was one of the hookers who frequented the club.

There was nothing to link Archibald to the earlier victims but now he was flagged as a potential suspect. If he knew Lockwood then he had at least some association with the vice scene, so it was feasible that he knew or had at least met the other dead women. If he'd trusted Lockwood enough to make her a partner in a lucrative racket then his links with hookers obviously went a bit further than a quick fumble in some alley, too. The Met decided that Kenneth Archibald was somebody they'd like to speak to. The 57-year-old was interviewed, but denied knowing Lockwood at all despite her having his phone number on a card in her apartment. Then for some reason his story changed dramatically; on April 27 he walked into Notting Hill police station and asked to speak to a detective. He'd changed his mind, Archibald told the astonished desk sergeant; he'd killed her and he wanted to confess.

It seemed that the killings might have been solved almost as soon as the presence of a serial killer had been identified. In many ways Archibald looked good as a suspect. He'd already been on the Met's radar because of his links with Lockwood. Now he told the Notting Hill cops how Lockwood had been killed, and when and where he'd thrown her body into the river. He'd met her outside the Chiswick pub, he said, then later argued with her about money and strangled her in a rage. His story wasn't perfect but the basics were a close enough match to the facts of the case. Archibald was charged with murder and detained. Not everyone was convinced though. Archibald was in poor health and had mental health issues – always a red flag when someone confesses to a murder. At his trial in June he changed his mind again, retracted his confession and said he'd made the whole thing up while depressed. The jury agreed and he was acquitted of Lockwood's murder. It's fairly certain that was the right decision, because the Stripper killings hadn't stopped with his arrest.

With two definite victims of a serial killer and two more possible the police had been taking steps to catch the killer in the act. All four bodies had been found in and around the Thames. Now patrols around the river were increased. If the killer was picking off his victims near the river the extra activity might deter him; if he was just dumping them there then better surveillance increased the chances of catching him in the act. The police were about to be disappointed on both counts.

Helen Barthelemy was a former circus performer from Blackpool, although her parents were French and Scottish. Aged 20, she had a criminal record in her home town from before she'd moved to London – she had been convicted of luring a man to a quiet spot with promises of sex, but instead he'd been slashed with a razor then robbed. Now Barthelemy herself had apparently been lured away and attacked. She had last been seen in a bar by one of her friends; Barthelemy had left her handbag there, saying she was just going out for a short while. She never came back. On April 24 – three days before Archibald's confession – her naked body was found in a lane near a sports field in Brentwood. This was a change in the pattern; her corpse was dumped well to the northwest of the earlier victims, and over a mile from the river. There was no doubt that she'd fallen victim to the same killer though. As well as the now familiar marks of ligature strangulation and the removal of her clothes she was a small, dark haired street prostitute who'd suffered from an STD.

As well as the similarities with the previous murders there were some new and interesting things about this corpse. Barthelemy's body was filthy, suggesting that it had been stored somewhere for a while between being stripped and dumped. Close examination of her skin also found thousands of tiny particles of paint. This was the type used for spraying cars and other metal objects and the microscopic flecks were in a rainbow of colors. The detectives suspected that she had been stored near a workshop where spraying was going on, and airborne paint particles had found their way into the improvised crypt and onto her skin. This didn't immediately pinpoint the place where the body had been kept – London has hundreds of small paint shops and light industrial premises – but it was something.

Now something else was suggested, too. Following Barthelemy's discovery a new detective joined the team, Detective Superintendent William Baldock. Baldock questioned the assumption that the victims had been strangled, and instead suggested something startling and horrifying. Many of the women had teeth knocked out, he said. Perhaps they'd been asphyxiated while performing oral sex and these weren't deliberate murders, but a deviant sex act gone wrong. Because fellatio was much more of a taboo subject than it is today this idea appalled many people. Could there be any truth in it? Not likely. A moment's thought suggests that any prostitute in this position had a simple way to resist – bite, hard. All of them still had enough teeth left to make the point quickly and brutally. Baldock's suggestion hit hard at the time but today it's really just a sign of how prudish people were only a couple of generations ago. If it wasn't in such a grim context it would even be amusing.

Other police suggestions were more helpful. Baldock wasn't the only new member of the team – the head of Scotland Yard Criminal Investigation Department, Commander George Hatherill, had now taken over the investigation. Hatherill knew the best source of information on the dead women was their fellow prostitutes and it was essential to break down the barrier of trust that kept them away from the police. In an attempt to do this he took a bold step – he publicly appealed for prostitutes to come forward, under a promise of anonymity, if they knew anything that might help. Hatherill pointed out that if the Stripper wasn't stopped it would be prostitutes who would die. If anyone had been forced to strip by a client, or assaulted by one, they should contact the Met immediately. It worked – to a point. Hatherill's appeal was made on April 28 and two days later 45 prostitutes – and 25 men

– had supplied information. None of it pin-pointed the Stripper's identity though, and Hatherill's warning about the risk to hookers was about to be proven accurate.

Just after five in the morning on July 14 a chauffeur, up early to get his car ready, found Mary Fleming's body propped against a garage door in a street in Chiswick. Like Barthelemy this corpse was over a mile from the Thames, this time to the north of the first discoveries. Fleming, a tough 30-year-old Glaswegian who'd been on the streets for a decade, was well known for taking no nonsense from difficult clients and would fight back savagely if threatened. She might have been small but she carried a knife and she'd used it before. If she'd pulled it this time it hadn't helped her. The evidence collected from her nude remains suggested she'd put up a struggle, but her assailant had stunned her with a powerful blow over the heart then strangled her. This time the pathologist was careful to examine her skin, looking for traces of paint. He found them. Fleming's body had spent time in the same place as the previous victim. There could be absolutely no doubt that they were the work of the same predator. Inquiries around the site of the gruesome discovery suggested that the chauffeur had barely missed getting a sight of the Stripper's vehicle – neighbors had heard a car reversing down the street minutes before he found the body.

The location where Fleming's body was dumped showed another change in tactics by the murderer. When the police had increased patrols around the river he had outsmarted them by leaving Barthelemy well to the north. That was enough to leave some people wondering how he had predicted the police response, and even to wonder if he had inside knowledge of what the Met were doing – speculation that would resurface years later when possible suspects were discussed. By leaving her where he did it was as if he was saying "I know how you're trying to catch me, and it won't work." There was a heavy police presence in Chiswick, though. Most of the detectives felt this was a deliberate taunt. It all added to the pressure. By now over 8,000 people had been interviewed in connection with the case and the press were calling for an arrest before anyone else died. The tabloids had also given the killer his nickname – "Jack the Stripper" was in the headlines.

The paint flecks were the final clue the police needed to announce that all the murders were the work of one man. If the same traces had been found on the earlier victims it would have confirmed that fact sooner, but it's probably not too surprising that nothing showed up. Figg is perhaps the most likely of the eight to have been killed by someone else; she died four years before the next victim and was the only one who wasn't found naked. If she were a victim of the Stripper he would have been developing his methods at the time. Why did he start stripping the bodies? The victims were unlikely to have undressed themselves – they were streetwalkers who did the "car trade." At the time a lot of their business was oral sex – which "nice girls" wouldn't do – and even if a client wanted full sex they would just lift their skirt and pull down their panties. No, the clothes had been removed by the killer. The chances are that it was to eliminate evidence. Perhaps he'd left semen on their clothes, and while DNA matching was unknown at the time it might have been possible to match blood groups. Clothing also picks up fibers and hair, and even in 1964 detectives could do a lot with evidence like that; the main tool used to analyze them is a microscope, and unlike DNA sequencing microscopes have been around for centuries. It makes sense that the Stripper would have removed the clothing before storing the bodies, as that reduced the chances of the police collecting evidence from where the bodies were found. Of course it also let paint settle on the skin, but the tiny droplets would have formed a thin, invisible mist in the air and it would take a very smart killer to think of that. The paint on the skin wasn't obvious; it took good forensic work to find it on Bathelemy and the later victims. If Rees was killed by the Stripper and stored in the same place it would have been difficult to find the clue after she'd spent weeks buried in a pile of garbage. Tailford and Lockwood had been thrown in a polluted river, and in Tailford's case she'd been

in the water for a week. Water and decay
would have removed a lot of the paint. It was
only when the Stripper altered his methods
and started abandoning corpses on dry land
that the clue started to show up. It would soon
show up again.

On October 23 Kim Taylor was working
with her friend Frances Brown, also known as
Margaret McGowan, near a pub in Notting Hill.
Events of the last months had made them
wary; like Mary Fleming and many other girls
they were carrying knives or sharpened steel
combs, but obviously that wasn't enough to
guarantee a girl's safety. Taylor and Brown had
decided to work as a pair for safety; that way,
they figured, the Stripper wouldn't be able to
pick them off. They'd been joking earlier in the
pub about the chances of meeting the killer,
but they both knew it wasn't a laughing matter. Back outside they were watching over
each other, casting suspicious glances at any
man who approached to talk.

When two cars pulled up at the same time
both girls took a good look at the one the other was getting into. Brown climbed into a Ford,

either a Zodiac or a Zephyr, and Taylor got into the other car. The vehicles soon split up in the London traffic. Taylor did what her client paid her to do, returned to the pub and waited for Brown to return. She never did.

It was over a month before Taylor found out what had happened to her friend. On November 25 Brown's body was found in Horton Street, Kensington, just outside an underground Civil Defense building. Unlike the other bodies, which were left in plain sight, Brown's had been partly concealed; dead branches and a dustbin lid had been piled on the corpse. Apart from that anomaly the marks of the Stripper were clear. She had been strangled and undressed, and her body was speckled with tiny particles of colored paint. She was also a short, dark-haired prostitute with a history of STD infection, but the nudity and paint settled it anyway. The Stripper had killed another one.

This time it wasn't just the victim's clothes that were missing. Some of Brown's jewelry was gone as well. When she vanished she had been wearing a gold ring and a silver cross on a chain, but these had vanished. They weren't the sort of items that would hold much evidence, and in fact they were risky things for the killer to have taken – they were identifiable, and if he'd been caught with them in his possession he would have had a hard time explaining how he came to have them. Stealing them was a risk that seemed out of character for the usually meticulous Stripper.

The first time most people heard about psychological profiling of serial killers was from the 1991 movie The Silence of the Lambs, but as a technique it's been in use since the 1940s. Scotland Yard were busily trying to build one for the Stripper. Police psychologists suggested that Brown's missing jewelry meant he might be collecting souvenirs from his victims. They also believed he was probably a shy man who seemed outwardly quiet. The small size of all the victims – none was taller than five feet two inches – suggested that he was small himself and chose targets he could easily overpower. Some of what the psychologists said could be useful in building a case once the Stripper was in custody, but it didn't do a lot towards finding him. Before a profile can be used to narrow down a list of suspects there has to be a list to work with, and the pool of men who might be the Stripper was huge. If anything Brown's death made it larger.

[2]

THE SAPPHIRE AFFAIR

Anatoliy Golitsyn was born in Piryatin, Ukraine, in August 1926. When he was seven his family moved to Moscow, and Anatoliy later became a cadet at a military school. He joined the Komsomol, the communist youth movement, aged 15, and four years later graduated to the Communist Party of the Soviet Union. That same year, 1945, he entered the Moscow School of Military Counter-Espionage. This school was run by Smiert Shpionam – "Death to Spies" – which is familiar as James Bond's old adversary, SMERSH. In 1946 Golitsyn graduated as a member of the KGB, the Soviet Union's pervasive and powerful intelligence agency. He quickly rose up the ranks and worked on important projects, including drawing up plans for a reorganization of the Soviet intelligence agencies. He worked as a KGB agent in Vienna and Helsinki, and studied advanced degrees at the University of Marxism-Leninism and the state schools for diplomacy and intelligence. In 1952 he met Stalin himself.

As a KGB officer Anatoliy Golitsyn was part of the USSR's unofficial aristocracy, enjoying a far higher quality of life than the mass of Soviet citizens. Of course he also had access to far more information, and perhaps that persuaded him that life could be even better elsewhere. Either way, on December 15, 1961 he appeared at the US Embassy in Helsinki with his wife and daughter and announced that he wanted to defect to the USA.

There was little chance of the CIA turning down a request by a KGB Major who had been so deeply involved in the planning of Soviet intelligence operations, and Golitsyn's offer was immediately accepted. The CIA sent him to Stockholm, from where he was quickly flown to

West Germany to have his story checked out. It soon became obvious that Golitsyn was who he claimed to be and he was moved on, this time to the USA. Once there he was debriefed by the CIA's head of counter-intelligence, James Jesus Angleton.

Angleton was then, and remains now, a deeply controversial figure. Talented at sniffing out Soviet spies within the KGB, he finally descended into what looks like paranoia and decided that Soviet penetration of the west was far greater than it really was. Illegal surveillance of US citizens and repeated claims that various western leaders were KGB agents finally weakened his credibility, but by then he had turned the CIA upside down in a fruitless search for a high-ranking mole that probably didn't exist. He was finally forced to resign in 1974 after accusing CIA Director William Colby, Secretary of State Henry Kissinger and President Gerald Ford of being Soviet agents.

That was 1974, though. In 1961 the situation was very different. Angleton hadn't yet developed the obsessions that made him so harmful to the CIA in later years; he was firmly focused on the very real threat of Soviet infiltrators in western intelligence agencies. Now here was a Soviet defector who claimed to know who many of them were. One of Golitsyn's first revelations struck close to Angleton himself.

Our Man in Beirut

Harold Adrian Russell "Kim" Philby was the eccentric son of a British Indian civil servant. He'd entered a career in journalism in the 1930s but by 1941 this had become a cover for a job with MI6, the British intelligence service. He'd first met Angleton in 1942, when the American had developed suspicions about his loyalty. Nevertheless by 1949 the two men had become friends, and when Philby was posted to Washington they met for lunch at least once a week.

It turned out that Angleton wasn't the only one who'd wondered who Philby was really working for. In May 1951 MI5 – the counter-intelligence and security service – planned to arrest two suspected Soviet spies who also happened to be friends of Philby. Before Guy Burgess and Donald Maclean could be lifted somebody warned them, and they escaped to Moscow via France. Suspicion instantly fell on Philby, who resigned from MI6 in protest. He denied any connection with the Soviets however, and was officially cleared in 1955. By this time he had gone back to journalism. In 1956 he moved to Beirut, Lebanon as a correspondent for The Observer and The Economist. In fact he had been re-employed by MI6, who were at least partly convinced of his innocence.

Now Golitsyn told MI6 that their early suspicions had been correct – Philby was indeed a KGB agent. Another MI6 officer interrogated him and Philby confessed everything, then fled to Moscow on a Soviet ship. It was a dramatic confirmation of Golitsyn's value to the west, and it instantly convinced Angleton that the defector should be listened to.

Plenty of people wanted to listen. Golitsyn had chosen the USA when he'd planned his defection, but the other main intelligence agencies wanted in on the game and the CIA were happy to cooperate. Intelligence sharing between the NATO allies has had its highs and lows, but in the early 1960s it was definitely at one of its peaks. The British were passing the CIA everything they got from their prize source Oleg Penkovsky, and even allowing CIA officers to meet him during his trips to the west. With the prickly de Gaulle back in power it was undesirable to upset the French by cutting them out, and there were advantages in letting the West German Bundesnachrichtendienst have access too. East Germany's master spy, Markus Wolf, had managed to infest the West German government with agents, and if Golitsyn could help the BND identify them so much the better.

The British had a large intelligence staff in the USA because they were running so many joint operations, but the other allies needed to fly in reinforcements. The SDECE's head officer in Washington was Philippe Thyraud de Vosjoli, and one morning in early June 1962 his phone rang at five in the morning. A French voice told him that six senior officers of the SDECE and the DST – the counter-intelligence service - had just landed at Washington airport; they needed to be collected. De Vosjoli was astonished, and his surprise only increased when the visitors arrived at the French embassy and told him why they were there. Golitsyn had revealed a Soviet plot that went right to the heart of the French government.

Source Protection

Golitsyn had established his credibility by confirming the suspicions about Philby. Now he started to reel off details of more Soviet agents. Of course in most cases he didn't have their names, or even much in the way of details.

Intelligence agencies work hard to recruit agents, but once they've done so it can often be very difficult to use the intelligence they supply. The problem is that acting on the information can often give the enemy the clues they need to identify the source of the leak. Painstaking secrecy is used to avoid this. The actual name of an agent is usually known to as few people as possible. Often only the team who handle the agent will know it; when they write their reports the agent is identified only by a code name or number. That's only the first and most basic precaution. Where possible the fact that the information even came from an agent will be concealed. A team that has recruited a senior member of a terrorist organization may write all their reports to make it appear the information is coming from a concealed microphone, for example. It can be very hard to decide when to act on intelligence reports. To intelligence officers the "circle of knowledge" is a key concept – the number of people on the other side who know a fact. It's always dangerous to use the intelligence you've collected, because to do so will tell the enemy that one of them is working for you. If the circle of knowledge is small the chances of them identifying the agent are much higher.

Even by intelligence standards the KGB took paranoia, mistrust and compartmentalization to extremes; constantly afraid of its own staff escaping across the Iron Curtain, the huge agency did everything it could to prevent officers learning any fact they didn't absolutely need to know. Golitsyn was a highly trained and trusted officer, though; a graduate of the higher intelligence school who'd been involved in restructuring agent networks and possessed a near-photographic memory. For the top men in Soviet intelligence his defection was the ultimate nightmare.

From a western point of view the Soviet agent networks inside NATO were like a huge jigsaw, with only scattered pieces visible. Golitsyn had managed to collect enough pieces that he could start joining them together and show glimpses of the true picture. He told Angleton that a CIA officer with an Eastern European background and a surname that began with K, and who had been posted to West Germany, was a Soviet spy codenamed "Sasha"; this sparked an obsession that came to dominate Angleton's later career.

Next the defector told MI5 that the KGB had a source inside the Admiralty, the headquarters of the Royal Navy. An investigation led to John Vassall, a civil servant who had access to thousands of classified documents and seemed to be living a more expensive lifestyle than his salary would support. Vassall was arrested and immediately confessed; the KGB had discovered he was gay, he told his interrogators – homosexuality was illegal in the UK at the time - and blackmailed him into supplying information. Aleksandr Kopatsky was a Soviet who had been recruited by the CIA in West Berlin; information provided by Golitsyn revealed that he was in fact a double agent who was still loyal to Moscow – and, very likely, he was "Sasha," the mole who Angleton turned the CIA inside out trying to find.

Golitsyn's revelations became more terrifying as time went on. He told the SDECE that a French NATO official was working for the KGB and was effectively treating NATO HQ as a Soviet library; any document the KGB wanted to see could be retrieved, copied and sent to Moscow within 48 hours. The penetration was so complete that the KGB section exploiting the information was using the NATO document reference system in their own paperwork. This claim seemed too incredible to be true and the SDECE decided to catch Golitsyn out. They brought in a stack of NATO documents and asked Golitsyn to tell them which ones he'd seen before. It was a carefully planned test; many of the documents were genuine but others were fakes, completely convincing but manufactured to check the defector's credibility. Golitsyn read through the documents and sorted them into three piles. Some of them he couldn't be sure about, he explained; that was the third pile. However he'd seen all the documents from this pile in Moscow, but none of these.

Every one of the files he claimed to have seen was genuine. Every one of the fakes was in the other pile.

The stunned SDECE agents could draw only one conclusion; Golitsyn was telling the truth. The investigation eventually led to Georges Pâques, a press officer at NATO HQ. French counter-intelligence officers followed him for nearly a year. Finally, in 1963, they burst into his apartment and arrested him in front of a guest. The guest was allowed to leave because he had immunity – he was a Soviet diplomat. Under interrogation Pâques confessed that he had been recruited by the USSR during the war, when he was based in de Gaulle's Free French headquarters in Algiers. Before going to work for NATO he had been an aide to the chiefs of staff in the Defense Ministry. He had been passing information to Moscow for nearly

19 years. In court Pâques argued that he had never been a Soviet agent and had merely been trying to prevent a nuclear war, but the court wasn't impressed and sentenced him to life in prison. Six years later he was released on the personal orders of de Gaulle.

Sapphire

Like Angleton and the British, the SDECE were now convinced that Golitsyn was the real deal. They were horrified when he told them Pâques wasn't the only traitor in France. In fact, the defector told them, there was a whole network of senior French officials working for the KGB. They were scattered throughout the intelligence services, the military, government ministries and even as high as the cabinet.

The French had known there were problems. Golitsyn had mentioned agents in France during his early interviews and the revelations were alarming enough that they were passed directly to President Kennedy. Kennedy wrote a personal letter to de Gaulle warning him of extremely high-level Soviet spies in the French government, and de Gaulle sent General de

Rougemont to Washington to check out the story. De Rougemont, one of the leading figures in French military intelligence, played it safe; he had no idea who might be working for the Soviets, so he stayed away from the embassy and SDECE staff. Even his friend de Vosjoli didn't know he was in the country. In fact de Rougemont was suspicious of everyone. He later told de Vosjoli that at first he thought the whole scheme was a treacherous plot by les Anglo-Saxons to attack de Gaulle's government. That idea didn't last long. After interviewing Golitsyn for three days he was shaken to the core. The defector's knowledge of the inner workings of the SDECE and French government was terrifying. It was clear that the KGB really did have sources deep inside the intelligence agency and close to de Gaulle himself. Returning to Paris, the general passed on what he'd learned. The response was the dispatch of the six-man team who woke de Vosjoli in early June.

At first de Vosjoli was irritated that a special team had been sent from Paris without any warning. Annoyance turned to shock when the senior man among the visitors explained why. The revelations in Kennedy's letter had been so shocking that nobody in SDECE knew who they could trust. Any message sent to de Vosjoli might be intercepted; even their most secure communications systems could no longer be depended on. De Rougemont, as one of de Gaulle's most trusted advisers, had slipped in and out of the USA without contacting any French staff who might be working for the enemy. Now this team was going to take over the debriefing of Golitsyn. Of course the information they gained would have to be sent back to France and there was a risk of it being seen by a Soviet agent. To disguise the defector's identity he would be given a codename by the SDECE; from now on anything supplied by Golitsyn would go out under the title Martel.

The news that there was a defector didn't come as a great surprise to de Vosjoli. As a senior intelligence officer he was part of a secretive community in Washington, a loose-knit group where secrets were the currency of business. Every agency had things it wanted to keep to itself, but even so they were all sitting on a lot of information that could be traded. The pieces of the intelligence jigsaw can be scattered among half a dozen organizations. Cooperation helps them all. Now de Vosjoli was picking up hints that the CIA had a new source of information on KGB operations in the west. Professionally curious, he tried to find out more. His American friends smiled and changed the subject, and he was only able to find a few tantalizing clues. Everything he learned was passed back to Paris, and predictably his superiors pressed him to find out all he could about the new source, especially his knowledge of KGB agents in France.

Then, abruptly, the orders changed. A terse message arrived from Paris. Stop asking questions, de Vosjolie was told. He was baffled. It wasn't until the debriefing team arrived that he understood – with de Rougemont on his way to the USA any further questions about the source could only complicate things. Of course he was still annoyed; the fact that the Americans had gone over his head by writing directly to de Gaulle, instead of passing a message through him, implied that he wasn't trusted.

Of course he was right; until the Soviet moles were identified nobody in the SDECE – or even the French government – could be trusted. It was about to get worse.

The French agents were allowed to debrief Golitsyn thoroughly, but because he'd defected to the USA there were American observers present during every session. As the KGB man poured out the details of his agency's penetration of France, de Vosjoli could feel the growing chill between the Americans and the French. Dismayingly, but predictably, the CIA were regarding the SDECE with increasing suspicion. Golitsyn knew that a senior SDECE officer was a Russian spy, but he didn't know who it was. That meant it could be any of them.

There was another, even greater worry. The KGB was one of the most effective intelligence agencies in history and highly skilled at building networks of agents. One spy inside the enemy's organization is in a very vulnerable position; a group of spies working together can cover each other's tracks. It's a lot harder to work out where the leak of information is because with multiple people supplying information it becomes almost impossible to pinpoint the desk that all the stolen secrets crossed. From the point of view of an organization as paranoid and distrustful as the KGB it also provided a way to check the reliability of their sources – material from one agent could be compared with others. This tactic made it very unlikely that there was only one Soviet agent in SDECE and the Americans were naturally worried.

It goes without saying that those inside the French intelligence services were suspicious of each other too. Some people were assumed to be safe – the chief of SDECE, General Paul Jacquier, was an air force officer who had only joined the organization after Golitsyn defected, so he couldn't be the top spy. De Vosjoli himself had been in Washington for years and the spy was known to be in Paris. Everyone else in SDECE was under a cloud of suspicion and that cloud darkened as the interviews went on. Golitsyn's information was explosive – and horrifying.

- A KGB cell, codenamed "Sapphire," was operating at a high level inside SDECE. It had over half a dozen members, all of whom had been directly recruited by the Soviets.
- The key ministries of the French government – defense, the interior and foreign affairs – all had KGB agents among their top officials.
- A member of President de Gaulle's cabinet was a Soviet spy. He had been part of de Gaulle's first cabinet in 1944, which suggested he must be among the French leader's most trusted colleagues.
- Worst of all, the members of the Sapphire network were manipulating SDECE into setting up a new team to spy on the USA's nuclear weapons program. Officially the purpose of this operation was to help France develop its own nuclear forces. In fact the real plan was to pass American

nuclear secrets to the USSR. It had been proposed in 1959 by KGB General Sakharovsky, head of the First Chief Directorate – the division of the KGB responsible for covert operations abroad.6

The team was collecting valuable information, and every night they sent a long report back to Paris in a unique code issued specifically for Martel material. At first the traffic was two-way. Paris supplied files on possible suspects and the interviewers described them to Golitsyn. The defector would use his knowledge to evaluate them, telling the French if they were likely candidates, possibilities or if a discrepancy ruled them out. With what they were learning, they thought, they should be able to clear out the infiltrators and identify the traitors who had turned against France. They even believed that they were building a case against the highest ranking of the spies, a man close to de Gaulle whose name still hasn't been revealed more than 50 years later. But slowly they began to realize that things were not going as they should.

As well as the distrust caused by the sheer scale of KGB operations in France the Americans were now growing worried at the apparent inaction of the French authorities. Hundreds of pages of information had been sent back to Paris, giving detailed descriptions of the agents. Despite this there had been no arrests or dismissals. Some of the Americans worried that the French weren't taking this seriously – perhaps they still believed it was an elaborate plot by the CIA. Others feared something much worse. Was the KGB network so extensive and powerful that it could shield its members even from a high level SDECE investigation? Things came to a head in early October 1962, when General Jacquier visited Washington. The Americans held a dinner in his honor at an exclusive club on F Street; the guest list was like a Who's Who of the US intelligence community. It should have been the social highlight of Jacquier's trip, but the atmosphere was poisoned by the deepening suspicions. Over dinner Jacquier was told politely but firmly that the CIA's patience was running out; enough information had been collected to start acting against Sapphire and the other networks, and it was time to start cleaning house. The implication was obvious – if the French didn't purge themselves of traitors the Americans would stop cooperating with them.

Jacquier was a military officer, brought in to SDECE for his leadership and management abilities. De Vosjoli was an intelligence professional and he recognized the seriousness of the threat. The French intelligence services were powerful and ruthless but their collection abilities were dwarfed by the CIA and NSA; if the Americans withdrew their cooperation France's security would be seriously endangered. It wouldn't end there either. If the Franco-American relationship broke down the British would certainly cut links too, both to preserve their own access to US secrets and to isolate themselves from a nest of spies. That would relegate the SDECE to a distant second place within Europe, which de Vosjolie found unacceptable. He worried that Jacquier wasn't taking it seriously enough; the general flew back to Paris with a lengthy report in his briefcase, but would he – could he – act on it? Before the situation could develop any further, though, a much larger crisis overshadowed it. For weeks America – and de Vosjoli - had been looking nervously at events in the Caribbean, and now a series of dramatic events drew all eyes to what was happening in Cuba.

[3]

THE CUBAN MISSILE CRISIS

By the early 1970s military strategists - in the west, at least - were moving towards the idea of "escalation"; any war between NATO and the Warsaw Pact would probably start off conventional, and might or might not escalate to chemical warfare, then tactical nuclear weapons and ultimately a strategic nuclear exchange. Soviet planners had a different view and saw chemical weapons and tactical nukes as tools for conventional warfighting, but both sides largely saw any potential conflict beginning with a land war – probably in Germany – and only escalating to global nuclear war in certain circumstances. There have been many novels about that war that never happened, such as Tom Clancy's Red Storm Rising, Harold Coyle's Team Yankee, Bob Forrest-Webb's Chieftains and General Sir John Hackett's The Third World War. All of them were written in the 1970s and 80s.

In the 1950s and 60s things were very different. Conventional land and naval forces were for proxy wars, or other conflicts where the superpowers didn't confront each other directly. If the USA and USSR did come to blows it would be in the form of a total nuclear war. The main weapons of that war would have been strategic bombers, intercontinental ballistic missiles (ICBMs) and from 1961 submarine launched ballistic missiles (SLBMs). The problem was that while all of these were capable of hitting cities or large bases, only the bombers had the accuracy to hit small, hard targets like missile silos and underground command centers. As air defenses became more sophisticated the chances of the bombers making it to their targets were plummeting, so planners increasingly had to rely on missiles – and that just wasn't good enough.

Even the megaton-range nuclear warhead hardened bunkers like the NORAD complex under Cheyenne Mountain, or the Russian equivalent at Zhiguli, were incredibly hard to destroy; Cheyenne Mountain was built – perhaps slightly optimistically - to survive a 30 megaton blast at a distance of 1.2 miles. Most warheads delivered less than 10 megatons, with the average weapon in 1962 having a yield of about 1.2Mt. To destroy a major command center, or a very hard target like a missile silo, multiple weapons would have to hit within half a mile. The problem was the guidance systems weren't good enough. Missile error is measured in CEP, or Circular Error Probable. This is the diameter of a circle that half of the warheads will land inside. The last US ICBM design was the MX Peacekeeper, which had a CEP of less than 400 feet, and the Trident II SLBM uses star sighting sensors to bring that down to about 300 feet (officially – the real figure is classified and possibly much better.) It was different in 1962 though. The first Soviet SLBM, the SS-N-4, carried a 1.2 Mt warhead and had a CEP of 2.5 miles; it had very little chance of destroying a hard target. At the time land based ICBMs were more accurate, but even they would have struggled to wipe out the enemy's headquarters and missile forces; the US Atlas missile could drop a 3.75 Mt warhead within 0.9 miles of the target, while the Soviet R-7A had a 2.9 Mt warhead and a CEP of 1.6 miles. Both sides were desperate to find a solution. In 1961 the USA came up with a simple one.

Ballistic missiles are steered by inertial guidance systems, which are programmed with the precise locations of the launch point and target. Gyroscopes and accelerometers constantly measure the missile's speed and direction, and steer it from one point to the other. The accuracy is never perfect though; tiny errors in the sensors and external factors like air density as they pass through the atmosphere gradually add up, and the missile is rarely exactly where its guidance computer thinks it is. A longer flight lets the errors grow larger, and the accuracy slowly degrades. From the missile fields in the American Midwest the distance to any Soviet target was at least 5,000 miles, and often much more. That allowed large errors to creep in.

It quickly became obvious to Strategic Air Command that the main problem was distance, and the way round it was simple – move the missiles closer to the USSR. In 1958 Strategic Air Command transferred 60 PGM-17 Thor Intermediate Range Ballistic Missiles (IRBMs) to Royal Air Force Bomber Command. These were deployed in the UK under "dual-key" control – both the UK and USA had to agree to launch. From UK sites the missiles could put a 1.44 Mt warhead on Leningrad in 18 minutes. Three years later more advanced PGM-19 missiles under direct SAC control were based in Italy and Turkey. Some of these were less than 400 miles from the bases of the Soviet Navy's Black Sea Fleet, or they could hit Moscow around 15 minutes after launch.

The deployment of IRBMs to Europe solved SAC's targeting problems, but it was to have serious effects on international relations. With an arc of SAC missile bases in Western Europe, Polaris missile submarines under the polar ice cap and B-52 bombers on Guam, the Soviet leadership could feel a nuclear noose tightening around their necks.

John F. Kennedy made "closing the missile gap" and catching up with the USSR part of his 1960 presidential platform, but in fact the missile gap was massive and the USSR was on the wrong side of it – they had a total of 3,600 nuclear weapons, and probably less than 40 ICBMs. The USA had 144 Atlas ICBMs, dozens of the new Minuteman I and a range of medium and intermediate range weapons as well as a growing SLBM force and a vast array of nuclear-armed bombers and tactical weapons; in total the US nuclear arsenal contained over 27,000 warheads. The Soviets were worried, and began frantically looking for a response.

The USA had a superior strategic position because NATO's European members were close to the western USSR, making it easy to reach Moscow, the Soviet leadership and most of the Russian population. There were also two independent but allied nuclear powers in Western Europe; one was France and the second was the UK, which as a matter of policy was adopting US nuclear weapons wherever possible.1 With Guam and, if necessary, South Korea to threaten the eastern USSR it was possible to attack high-value targets throughout the country with accurate short-range weapons, and keep the ICBM force for a follow-on strike against larger, more vulnerable objectives. The USSR's position was much weaker. The USA only has two land borders; to the north is Canada – a fellow NATO member – and to the south Mexico, which had a moderate leftist government that was not friendly to the USSR. There was no chance of establishing missile bases anywhere in North America, so the only remaining choice was on an island in the Caribbean. Unfortunately for Moscow most of these are former British or French colonies, and tended to have strong links with Western Europe. There was one exception though – Cuba.

---

[1] If the Soviets had detected an incoming US nuclear weapon – especially a Polaris or, later, Trident II SLBM – they would have had no way of knowing who had launched it, and would have had to assume it was the beginning of a US strike against them. The unofficial policy of Britain's strategic forces during the Cold War was "We don't have to be able to *win* a nuclear war; we just have to be able to *start* one."

Until 1958 Cuba had been ruled by Fulgencio Batista, a pro-US but unpopular dictator. On January 1 1959, after a six-year insurgency, Batista was overthrown by Fidel Castro's revolutionaries. At first the USA welcomed the change, as they had been increasingly annoyed by Batista's brutal rule and links with organized crime, but when Castro legalized the Communist Party and started shooting Batista supporters relations quickly soured. By 1960 Cuba was rapidly drifting into the Soviet sphere of influence. The Kremlin recognized an opportunity, which only became more tempting as the USA launched repeated attempts to overthrow or assassinate Castro. In early 1962 premier Nikita Khrushchev persuaded the Cuban revolutionary that his best defense against US attacks would be a strong Soviet military presence on the island, a presence that would include a powerful battery of IRBMs. Launched from Cuba these missiles could hit targets anywhere in the continental USA, turning them into a strategic force. Additional medium range missiles, able to strike most of the eastern seaboard, would also be deployed. It seemed the perfect counter to the US missiles in Europe, especially if the missiles could be brought in under strict secrecy. Nobody in Moscow or Havana anticipated that they were about to push the world to the very edge of nuclear war.

Penkovsky

The KGB wasn't the only intelligence agency operating in the Soviet Union. The military had its own service, which focused on collecting information about foreign armed forces and their equipment. Lower profile than the KGB, the Chief Intelligence Directorate of the General Staff – the GRU – was regarded by many western agencies as an even more dangerous adversary. It also had even tighter security, and the west had much more trouble penetrating it than they did with the KGB. There were some successes though.

One day in July 1960 two American students from Indiana University, in Moscow to practice their Russian, were returning to their hotel from an evening out at the Bolshoi Theater. As they crossed the Bolshoi Moskvoretsky Bridge, admiring the view of the Kremlin towers, Russian pedestrians walked by, most of them conspicuously ignoring the foreigners – anyone could be watching, and talking to an American could result in detention and interrogation by the KGB's counter-espionage service. One Russian was willing to take the risk though. As he weaved through the foot traffic he quickly shoved a package into a student's hands then walked on without a word. It was done so quickly and professionally that nobody could have seen a thing. The astonished student quickly concealed the package, then examined it later back in his hotel room. There was no clue to what it contained and, unsure what to do with it, he handed it in at the US Embassy and explained how he'd come to have it. It quickly found its way to the CIA station chief.

The package turned out to be from a senior GRU officer, Colonel Oleg Penkovsky, and he was offering to pass information to the CIA. To establish his credentials he included the names of 18 GRU officers working undercover in the

USA.7 It was an unprecedented chance to penetrate the secretive organization and the CIA should have jumped at it. Instead they hesitated. Apparently they believed that they were under constant surveillance and feared being caught in a KGB trap. Penkovsky knew who the KGB's watchers were following, though, and when the CIA didn't get back to him he approached Greville Wynne. Wynne was a British businessman who owned an engineering company, and he sold his products throughout Eastern Europe. The business was completely genuine, and made Wynne large amounts of money. It was also an ideal cover for travel inside the Warsaw Pact. In fact Wynne had been recruited to MI5 before the war and transferred to MI6 sometime in the 1950s. In 1959 he had helped a KGB officer to defect to the west. Now Penkovsky repeated his offer, and Wynne was willing to take the chance. He arranged for Penkovsky to meet MI6 and CIA officers during a visit to London on April 21, 1961. This was just a formality though. By then a transfer system had already been set up through MI6 in Moscow, to allow the Russian to pass information to his handlers.

Ruari Chisholm was an underpaid and over-worked visa officer at the British Embassy in Moscow. Every day he went to work in the old building, the pre-Communist offices of the Rossiya Insurance Company, that stood direct-ly across the Moskva River from the Kremlin. Stalin had hated it; every morning when he looked out the window of his office he'd seen the Union Flag fluttering, defying him. Stalin was dead now but the Soviets were still nerv-ous of the Embassy. They doubted all the an-tennas on the roof were there to listen to Radio Moscow. Chisholm claimed it was a bor-ing place to work, though. All he did all day, he complained at diplomatic parties, was stamp passports. Meanwhile his wife Janet enjoyed sitting in Moscow parks watching their three children play. Sometimes locals would con-gratulate her on her offspring. Occasionally they would even offer her small gifts; fruit, or maybe candy.

Some of these gifts were handed over by Penkovsky. In fact Ruari Chisholm was the chief of the MI6 Moscow Station, the senior British intelligence officer inside the USSR. His wife had plenty of experience at passing messages back and forward between her husband and the agents he controlled, and now she was the go-between for the GRU colonel.

Penkovsky's career as a British agent would span only 14 months. He worked too hard and took too many risks to last long. In just over a year he handed Janet Chisholm photographs of over 5,000 secret documents and named more than 300 Soviet agents in the west. Then, as the USA started to become suspicious of the new Soviet bases in Cuba, Penkovsky began passing details on the USSR's nuclear missile forces.

The USA was getting reports from Cuban émigrés in Florida about what looked suspiciously like missile launch facilities.8 US spy planes constantly observed the construction sites – and provoked diplomatic complaints from Cuba – but they didn't know enough about Soviet missile bases to positively identify them. Now Penkovsky handed over the information they needed. He told his contacts exactly what was required to support each model of Soviet missile, and how the bases would be laid out. By early October US Air Force and CIA analysts had applied this information to their photos of Cuba and identified no less than nine ballistic missile bases. All they needed to locate now were the missiles themselves.

Eyes on the Ground

The resolution of modern surveillance satellites is highly classified but extremely impressive – it's not possible to read a vehicle license plate from space, of course, but you can certainly tell if the vehicle has a license plate. Technology hadn't got that far in the early 60s though. The photos of Cuba that were coming in from satellites and the U-2 spy planes – one of which was shot down by a Soviet missile on October 279 - provided a lot of information, but their ability to show small details was limited. During the Cold War there was also a shroud of secrecy around Soviet military equipment. Western analysts often knew little about new systems for years after they first appeared and military manuals were written on little more than a few grainy photos, descriptions from refugees and educated guesswork. The Soviets played games with NATO observers, too. The annual military parade in Moscow's Red Square was one of the best chances to see the USSR's latest military equipment, and western diplomats – many of them intelligence officers – turned up in force with their cameras. Some of the impressive weaponry trundling past was fake, though – at least one "missile system" is known to have been just an empty tube on the back of a truck.10 At the same time some real systems never appeared on the parade and others were modified to confuse analysts. Simply spraying a shoe box with green paint and gluing it to a tank's turret could spark a year-long study by MI6 or the CIA to work out what it was – Was it a laser rangefinder? A chemical weapon detector? An air conditioning system that could mean the Red Army was preparing for a war in the Middle East? Russians are historically very good at maskirovka – creating a false picture and showing it to the enemy – and the Soviet general staff's Office of Strategic Deception took it to new heights. The west often had a very sketchy idea of what Soviet military equipment looked like and what it could do.

The Soviet missiles that Penkovsky said were heading for Cuba were launched from fixed sites, but for travel they could be loaded onto huge trailers and towed. Of course they weren't the only Soviet missiles that could be towed around. There were already SA-2 "Guideline" anti-aircraft missiles on Cuba, and they were also moved around on trailers. The SA-2 was extremely large for a SAM and confusion was easily possible. Ask any military intelligence expert what it's like interviewing civilians about military equipment and you better be prepared to hear a long list of frustrations. The most common problem is with armored vehicles – anything that has armor around the sides, a gun on top and a green paint job will be described as a tank. Missiles are also close to the top of the list. To most people a big rocket on a trailer is a big rocket on a trailer, and they just don't notice the differences that would let an expert tell whether it was a ballistic missile or a SAM. That's an important distinction. SAMs are defensive weapons, and the Guidelines could only hurt Americans if they were flying over Cuba. The R-12 and R-14 missiles were offensive systems, though. As October went on the CIA were overwhelmed with confusing reports from the island, and they had no way to make sense of them. Most of their sources on the island had died or fled during the purges that followed Bautista's fall and they were too reliant on the photographs. Then de Vosjoli offered to help.

As early as July the Frenchman had been hearing about unusually large numbers of Soviet ships docking at the Cuban port of Mariel. In August – before General Jacquier's visit – he flew to Havana himself. De Vosjoli believed that France and the USA had the same basic interests, and he was keen to share information. Before he left he spoke to CIA Director John McCone, and he was also relying on his general orders for legal cover. These orders didn't mention Cuba specifically, but they did tell him to cooperate with the Americans wherever this was in the interests of France. The SDECE man believed this was exactly such a case.

The Caribbean is scattered with former French colonies and overseas regions of France, so de Vosjoli already had the foundations of a network. French officials and expats regularly travelled to and from Cuba, and now de Vosjoli began seeking them out. He questioned everyone he could find who had been travelling around the island. If they'd seen Soviet military equipment he wrote down their descriptions. Where he could, he recruited people who were willing to go and take another look. Intelligence officers draw a clear line between sources who can be given instructions – they're called "taskable" sources – and those who aren't. Anyone can potentially give valuable information, but a taskable source can be told what to look for then sent out to report if they see it or not. De Vosjoli quickly built a network of both types. Soon he was getting between fifty and a hundred reports a day, from a stable of sources which expanded to include Cuban as well as French agents. It

didn't take long for him to strike intelligence
gold.

One of the people he spoke to was a former NCO in the French Army who had served
with NATO forces.11 This man had noticed Soviet military vehicles moving around and had
paid attention to it. Among the equipment
he'd seen, he told the SDECE man, were multi-
axle transporters carrying large missiles. The
weapons themselves were covered by tarpau-
lins, he said, but they were much larger than
SAMs. In fact they were larger than the American IRBMs he had seen in Europe. He'd seen
both SAMs and ballistic missiles and knew the
difference; he was sure.

Armed with this information de Vosjoli
could confirm to Paris that the Soviets were
building a nuclear missile base from which they
could threaten the entire eastern coast of the
USA – and, of course, France's possessions in
the Caribbean. Playing the Washington game
of quid pro quo he could also pass on what
he'd learned to the Americans – and he did.
Combined with the reconnaissance photographs and what they'd learned from Penkov-

sky it was enough to confirm all of the US government's fears.

The Crisis Erupts

So far the whole drama – the construction of the bases, the US efforts to find out what was happening and the movement of the missiles themselves – was happening under the tightest secrecy that could be arranged. With the missile bases confirmed the USA was determined to act; the question was how. Plans were drawn up for military strikes against the bases, but there were risks involved. The US military was operating close to home and could bring overwhelming force to bear against the Soviet outpost, but Penkovsky had discovered something else. As well as the ballistic missiles the Soviets on Cuba also had a number of 2K6 Luna missile launchers. Developed as heavy rocket artillery for Soviet tank armies these weapons, called FROG-5 by NATO, carried a nuclear warhead but had a range of only 28 miles. From Cuba the only US soil they could threaten was the naval base at Guantanamo Bay, but they could devastate any attempt to invade the island. The threat was a very real one. Penkovsky revealed that the Soviet commander on the island, General Pliyev, had been authorized to launch them against an invasion without requesting permission from Moscow. Any attempt to land troops on Cuba would fail on the beach in a storm of nuclear fire.12

As well as the obstacles to an invasion there was dissent at high levels in the USA. The Joint Chiefs believed that the missiles altered the strategic balance and made an invasion necessary; defense secretary Robert McNamara disagreed. McNamara thought that the US lead in nuclear weapons was so massive that an extra 40 Soviet warheads being moved within range made no difference. President Kennedy was caught in the middle. He accepted McNamara's argument, but felt that the appearance of a change in the balance of power was important too. He was also now aware of the nuclear threat to any invasion force. Finally he decided to pursue a diplomatic solution. At first he tried to resolve it in private with Soviet foreign minister Andrei Gromyko, but when Gromyko refused to remove the weapons, insisting they were for defensive purposes, Kennedy opted to go public. On October 14 he announced that the USA would not permit the USSR to build offensive bases on Cuba. The Soviets refused to back down, however, and by October 19 both sides were raising the alert levels of their nuclear forces. On the 22nd Kennedy announced to the nation that any nuclear missile launched from Cuba would trigger a full-scale retaliation against the USSR. There was no way the Soviets could stand firm; they knew – and so did Kennedy – that while they could damage the USA in a nuclear war they couldn't defeat it, while in return they would be completely destroyed.

For most of the human race it was a terrifying experience; in a matter of days the world had gone from a tense but apparently secure peace to a spiraling confrontation that seemed likely to end in nuclear war. Nuclear-armed aircraft and submarines were already skirmishing around the Caribbean; USAF carried nuclear-tipped air to air missiles and a US Navy helicopter dropped practice depth charges on a Soviet submarine, not knowing that it carried a nuclear torpedo and was authorized to launch it at a US fleet if attacked. Luckily the submarine's commander chose not to fire the weapon.

Of course neither side actually wanted to initiate World War 3, and behind the scenes diplomacy was going on at a frantic pace. Finally, on October 27, a secret agreement was reached between the superpowers. Publicly the USSR would back down and remove the missiles from Cuba. In return the USA would deactivate its own missiles in Italy and Turkey, and remove them within two years. Kennedy also gave a guarantee that the USA would never attempt to invade Cuba.

There were many repercussions from the Cuban missile crisis. The world was made aware as it never had been before how easily a nuclear war could be provoked. Both superpowers were aware that the search for a solution had been badly hampered by the difficulties of communicating between Washington and Moscow. To prevent the same problems happening again the famous "hot-line" was set up, giving the US and Soviet leaders a direct link that would remain open even during a crisis.

There were tragedies too. Oleg Penkov-sky's reports on Soviet nuclear forces had giv-en Kennedy the confidence he needed to make Khrushchev blink first, but in getting them to his handlers he'd taken too many risks. Jack Dunlap, a treacherous US Army sergeant work-ing at the NSA, saw reports that could only have come from a high-ranking GRU officer and passed them to his KGB handler. Penkov-sky was arrested at the height of the crisis, on October 22 1962. His contact Janet Chisholm and her husband Ruari were declared persona non grata and expelled from the USSR. Greville Wynne, the British agent who had recruited him, was an "illegal," operating under cover, and didn't have the diplomatic protection the Chisholms did; he was arrested in Budapest, brought back to Moscow and charged with spying. On May 11, 1963 he was sentenced to three years in prison followed by five in a labor camp;13 in 1964 he was exchanged for Konon

Molody, a KGB agent who had infiltrated the USA and UK by posing as a Canadian, "Gordon Lonsdale." Penkovsky was found guilty along with Wynne and executed a week after the trial. It's likely he was shot in the back of the head, the usual Soviet execution method, but there are persistent rumors that he was tied to a stretcher and fed into a crematorium alive.

Repercussions

With the missile crisis winding down de Vosjoie returned to the issue of Martel and his exposure of the KGB networks in France. All through the crisis the SDECE and CIA had kept on working with Golitsyn, slowly narrowing down the list of potential spies. To de Vosjoli's increasing dismay, though, there was still nothing happening back in France. It was as if the government had lost interest. Even within SDECE things were changing. He'd discussed it at length with General Jacquier, but his chief's attitude was shifting; now he seemed more influenced by his aides and less willing to listen to the reports from Washington. De Vosjoli kept pushing for action, but his own relations with Paris were becoming chilly. Finally, in early December, Jacquier summoned him back to Paris for an urgent meeting. When he got there he was told to see Colonel Mareuil, the officer in charge of cooperation with foreign agencies.

Mareuil had two requests for de Vosjoli. The first was to hand over a list of his sources in Cuba. De Vosjoli refused; protecting his sources was important to him, and there was no need for Mareuil to know the names. Already the meeting wasn't going well, and it was about to get a lot worse. Mareuil delivered his second request; de Vosjoli was to set up a team to steal secret US technology, to help France build its own nuclear force.14

De Vosjoli was stunned. This was exactly what Golitsyn had warned him of months ago – a plot to get nuclear weapon information from their allies, allegedly to develop French weapons. It was final proof, if he needed it, that the defector was telling the truth. Again he refused, hoping that when he met Jacquier the next day he would be able to resolve both issues.

He was in for a big disappointment. Instead of being given a chance to explain his concerns he came under a ferocious personal attack from several senior SDECE staffers before he even met the general. They accused him of exceeding his authority by passing information on the Cuban missiles to the Americans, despite his orders allowing him to do exactly that. Then it got worse. He'd misled his superiors, he was told, seriously increasing the risk of nuclear war; the SDECE were now satisfied that the missiles had only been SAMs2 – there had never been ballistic missiles on Cuba at all. De Vosjoli had helped the Americans manipulate de Gaulle into supporting Kennedy, which had harmed the relationship between France and the USSR. Finally, unable to take the abuse any more, de Vosjoli stormed into Jacquier's office and asked what was going on. He point-

---

[2] This accusation was complete nonsense. As well as the reports from de Vosjoli's sources on Cuba, photographs taken at the time have been re-examined with modern image analysis techniques. There were definitely Soviet ballistic missiles on Cuba in October 1962.

ed out that not only had Jacquier known what he was doing on Cuba, he'd written to him after the crisis was over to congratulate him on his work. It was useless though. Jacquier seemed to be a changed man; he simply mumbled something about de Gaulle having been left no choice but to support the Americans. Later that day it emerged that the British and Americans had just signed a deal on sharing nuclear technology; it was a sign of the special relationship at the heart of NATO, and de Gaulle and his sycophants were furious about it. Jacquier explained that de Gaulle – and thus the SDECE – no longer regarded the USA as an ally.

De Vosjoli was fuming when he returned to Washington, but he kept on doing his job as well as he could. Increasingly his freedom of action was being restricted though. The last thing he'd been told before flying back from France was that a new officer would be joining his team. This man's job would be to collect information on US strategic weapons. Worst of all, the information he would be looking for wasn't just technical; he was also to find the locations and planned targets of the American missiles.15 This would be of no use at all for the development of a French nuclear deterrent – but it would be extremely valuable to the Soviets. De Vosjoli tried one last time to remind his superiors of Martel's warning, but he was told to be quiet and follow orders.

In early February 1963 one of his Cuban sources sent him the latest order of battle for all the communist forces on Cuba. De Vosjoli passed it on to Paris. Immediately a reply came back – he was to supply the name of the agent who had sent him the document. As before de Vosjoli refused, but this time Jacquier himself repeated the demand. Unable to say no to the head of his agency, he supplied the name. The next report from Cuba told him that his agent had disappeared, arrested by Castro's feared secret police.

It just got worse. Not long after he was ordered to cut off contact with his Cuban network and stop working on the island. He asked who would be replacing him; there was no answer. Then an American friend passed him one of the last reports delivered by Penkovsky before his arrest. It was forwarded to Paris and promptly ignored, to the fury of the CIA. In June the Swedish air attaché, Colonel Wennerström, was arrested and charged with spying for the USSR. De Vosjoli began an investigation on several French officers who had been close friends of the Swede, but was abruptly ordered to drop it. Finally in September he was told that he was being replaced and should leave the USA on October 18. Georges Pâques, the NATO press officer, had been arrested the month before. He was one of the most senior civil servants in France and had worked closely with every post-war prime minister and president – but he'd been a Soviet agent since 1944.

Because the NATO headquarters was multinational several agencies had been looking for the spy within it; that may explain why Pâques was caught. He was the only French agent described by Golitsyn who was ever unmasked. All the others were in positions where the investigation would be entirely in French hands, and not one of those investigations paid off. De Vosjoli was left with a strong feeling that the Soviet agents in his homeland had gained so much power they were now un-touchable. His own agency appeared to be actively shutting down every attempt to find the traitors in its high command. For a loyal professional like de Vosjoli it was too much to take. He stayed at his desk until his replacement arrived, then resigned from the SDECE.

[4]

FACT AND FICTION

It's easy to understand why de Vosjoli felt betrayed. He'd dedicated twenty years of his life to his country, then been forced out in a move that looked very much like a ploy to protect enemy agents. Now he was bitter, and he didn't mind telling his friends why. Many of those friends were in Washington, and most were members of the NATO intelligence community. Most – but not all.

Leon Uris was born in Baltimore in 1924. His parents were first-generation Jewish immigrants – his father from Poland, his mother from Russia – and had links to the Zionist movement in Palestine. Young Leon was brought up on old stories of the Eastern European ghettoes, and developed a fascination for Jewish history and the Zionist cause. He wasn't an outstanding student – he never graduated high school and failed English three times – but he did like to write. His studies came to an end in his senior year when the Japanese launched their surprise attack on Pearl Harbor. Aged 17, he enlisted in the United States Marine Corps and spent the next four years as a radio operator in the Pacific; he saw combat at Guadalcanal and Tarawa. Later, sick with malaria, he met and married a female USMC sergeant.

After the war Uris drifted into journalism, writing for a local newspaper. In 1959 Esquire magazine bought one of his articles. That spurred him to take writing more seriously and he began work on his first novel, Battle Cry. Based on his own experiences as a Marine it quickly became a best seller and went on to become a popular movie. More books followed, including his most famous work, Exodus, in 1959. Telling the story of Jewish migration to Palestine from the late 19th century until the founding of Israel in 1948, it's still regarded as a classic of historical fiction.

Uris had made a name for himself by writing gripping novels based on thorough research and historical accuracy. He'd also got to know many people in the diplomatic community because of his knowledge of Israel, gained during an extended stay there in the mid-50s. Of course that meant he also knew many people in the intelligence community – many diplomats, especially in a major capital like Washington, are actually intelligence officers under "legal" cover. His work and experience had gained him status as a privileged outsider, who didn't have access to the real secrets but did get included in a lot of insider gossip. When his French friend started describing his frustration at what had happened to him he was fascinated.

Of course writing an exposé of the Sapphire affair would have closed a lot of doors – his contacts in intelligence would have seen it as a betrayal of their trust for journalistic motives. Turning it into a novel was different though. A dramatized account of the affair would be understood by those in the know but wouldn't compromise sources or cover stories.

The Novel

Uris published Topaz in 1967. The story took all the strands of the Sapphire affair and wove them into a fast-moving plot. The heroes of the novel were French agent André Devereaux and NATO intelligence expert Michael Nordstrom.

In the novel Devereaux and Nordstrom uncover the plot to ship missiles to Cuba and report it to their superiors. At first Devereaux is puzzled when nobody acts, but then he is targeted by assassins and realizes that he's stumbled into a Soviet operation that's far deeper even than the missile crisis.

With the assistance of a small group of anti-Castro Cubans and Soviet defectors the two struggle to track down the KGB's agents within NATO and France, while trying to get photographic evidence of the missiles in Cuba. Devereaux enlists his Cuban lover Juanita to get the vital photos, but she is killed soon after handing them over. Nordstrom tells Devereaux that a spy ring known as Topaz is operating inside the French intelligence services and gives him the name of a French NATO official, Henri Jarré, who is passing information to Moscow.

Returning to France, Devereaux finds that his wife has heard of his affair in Cuba and left him for Jacques Granville, another intelligence officer. Jarré dies in a staged suicide. Finally it is revealed that Granville is the leading Soviet agent, and faced with arrest he too kills himself.

The novel was a moderate success in the USA, spending 52 weeks on the New York Times bestseller list (although it spent only one week in the number one slot.) It was never released in France, though – the picture it painted of French-American relations was too bleak.

Enter Hitchcock

For Hitchcock the sixties were, in general, a pretty good decade. They opened with the massive success of Psycho, one of the most successful black and white films of all time, and it was quickly followed by The Birds. He wasn't without his failures though, and the 1964 psychodrama Marnie saw box office takings slip. It was still a success, but not on the scale producers had come to expect from Hitchcock, and it left him open to pressure from the studios. The cold war was at its height and people wanted spy dramas; Universal Studios persuaded Hitchcock to make two. The first was Torn Curtain, in 1966, starring Paul Newman as a fake defector, which became the third best earning movie of Hitchcock's career. The second was Topaz.

Creative Tension

When Universal asked Hitchcock to bring Topaz to the screen he immediately hired Uris to write the screenplay for him. There are advantages in this; the author of a novel understands the plot better than anyone else and can make the changes needed for a successful movie without losing any of the story's essential elements. Unfortunately there are some pitfalls as well.

It soon became clear that Uris and Hitchcock had different opinions about several aspects of the screenplay. Hitchcock was already well known for his black humor, and he wanted to inject some of it into the script. Uris disagreed; he wanted to concentrate solely on the dramatic elements. Hitchcock also felt the story was too black and white. The villains, he decided, were too one-dimensional and didn't come across as real people. He wanted Uris to add some humanity to them. Uris thought they were fine as they were. The disagreements quickly escalated until finally Uris left the project, leaving only a partial script behind.16

Next Hitchcock turned to Arthur Laurents, who had worked with him on Rope in 1948. Laurents refused, however, and the scheduled shooting dates were rapidly approaching. Finally Samuel A. Taylor, who had helped with the screenplay for Vertigo, agreed to step in. It was late in the day to be starting with a new writer but there was no choice. It was one of the few times in Hitchcock's long career that he began filming without a finished script to work from. That was doubly unfortunate because he had plans to experiment during this production, mostly by altering color balances to set moods during key scenes.

When shooting began the script still wasn't finished; some scenes were filmed within hours of being written. This gave parts of the movie a confused look, often very unlike the meticulously planned action Hitchcock was known for. At the same time it did have some technically brilliant set pieces, including one scene where a dying woman's dress spreads on the floor as she falls to give the impression of a growing bloodstain. Some of the confusion eventually caused serious problems for the team, though. To work well any thriller needs a well-plotted ending, and this was where Topaz had its biggest troubles. Most of the movie was shot on location, adding to the budget and time pressures. The main locations were Washington, DC, New York, Denmark, West Germany and France.

The End

Towards the end of filming Hitchcock had to return to the USA to attend to a family emergency – his wife had been suddenly taken ill. While he was gone Herbert Coleman, the associate producer, shot the ending scene that Hitchcock had developed. In it Granville and Devereaux fight a duel in a football stadium. This ending was shown during the first test screenings, but didn't go down well with audiences. The studio asked Hitchcock to come up with a new ending, which he promptly did. In this Granville escapes to the USSR at the end; footage of him boarding an Aeroflot flight to Moscow is intercut with scenes of Devereaux and his wife climbing the steps of a Pan Am flight to the USA. This also met with mixed reviews; some audience members found it confusing and were apparently unable to tell who was supposed to be flying where. Hitchcock liked it, but Universal asked for yet another change. In the final version Granville, exposed at a NATO meeting, goes home and commits suicide by jumping from a window. Because filming had already finished this ending was assembled from unused footage and, as there was no scene of Granville jumping and actor Michel Piccoli was no longer available, a new scene was shot in which he jumped behind drawn curtains.

Universal were happy with the new ending, but Hitchcock was not. He much preferred the second one and there was a bitter dispute between the two. The final decision was to use both. The main release would use the scene of Granville committing suicide. In the UK, however, test audiences had responded much better to Hitchcock's favorite; in Britain it would be released with that one. The original conclusion with the duel was dropped; for years it was thought the footage had been lost, until Hitchcock's daughter Patricia found it among his personal effects and donated it to the Academy of Motion Picture Arts and Sciences.

Unlike the novel it was based on the film was released in France, with a new name. To avoid confusion with the 1951 classic Topaze it was renamed L'Étau, meaning "the stranglehold," and the name of the spy ring was changed to Opal; the gemstone theme taken from the original Sapphire was maintained. The movie was a lot more successful in France than it had been in the USA: Often counted among Hitchcock's rare flops, it failed to regain its production costs at the US box office. Many critics blamed this on the lack of a big name Hollywood actor, and some went as far as to speculate that Hitchcock had intended to create his own star using the movie as a vehicle. He'd done this before with actress Tippi Hedren, whose career only really took off after she started working with Hitchcock, but if that was his plan this time it failed. Frederick Stafford, who played Devereaux, did well in the role but showed no signs of true greatness.

Topaz did feature a number of non-US stars, including three big names in the French movie industry – Philippe Noiret, Michel Piccoli and female lead Claude Jade. That might explain part of its success in France, but much of the credit for that has to go to Hitchcock himself – the French have always been admirers of his work. Of course the attraction of the story can't be overlooked either – Many French people felt they were being marginalized on the political scene, and Topaz put them back at the center of it.

CONCLUSION

Hitchcock's movie was released with two endings that each tied up the affair in a neat bow. For British audiences the leader of the spy network escaped to Moscow, as the Cambridge traitors Philby, Burgess and Maclean had done a few years earlier. In the US and French release rough justice was served – he killed himself after being unmasked and accused. What really happened to the members of Sapphire? The simple fact is that we don't know.

For much of 1962 and 1963 the SDECE threw a lot of resources at extracting information from Golitsyn, and they should have been able to work out who most of the Soviet agents were. Only one – the NATO mole Georges Pâques – was ever arrested, though, and even he was pardoned and released with almost indecent speed. Was Pâques the cabinet-level spy in the French government? It's possible – he had been close to de Gaulle for decades, since the days of the Free French government in exile during the war. Of course he'd been spying for Moscow all that time, and had been close to the center of the French Republic for 19 years. It could hardly have been more damaging if de Gaulle himself had been working for the Soviets.

Golitsyn also reported that there were spies in all the key ministries of the French government; none of them were ever unmasked. Nor was the network inside the SDECE – the Sapphire ring itself. As de Vosjoli quickly discovered when he tried to identify the traitors no action was allowed that might have exposed KGB influence so deep in the Paris government. Was it misplaced pride in the incorruptibility of French officials? That seems hard to believe. De Vosjoli himself thought it was something far more sinister – that the networks were so extensive they could block any attempt to expose them, and ultimately turn the SDECE itself against the USA in the service of the Soviet regime. Hitchcock often directed films with fantastic plots, but in the case of Topaz the reality seems more incredible than the fiction.

READY FOR MORE?

We hope you enjoyed reading this series. If you are ready to read similar stories, check out other books in the *Stranger Than Fiction* series:

THE TRUE STORY BEHIND ALFRED HITCHCOCK'S PSYCHO

For movie buffs Alfred Hitchcock will always be associated with a long list of Hollywood classics. Between 1921 and 1976 the English director known as the Master of Suspense released 52 feature films, many of which are still thrilling new audiences today. To most people, though, he's best known for a film that was very different – Psycho.

The most fascinating part of movie, however, is actually the real story behind it. This book tells the chilling true story behind of the movie.

THE TRUE STORY BEHIND ALFRED HITCHCOCK'S THE BIRDS

The Birds was different from most of Hitchcock's work. For admirers of Hitchcock The Birds also raises disturbing questions about the director as a person. He was a complex and confusing character in many ways, and perhaps it's not surprising that someone who built a career out of creating suspense and fear on screen might also have had some darker sides to his personal life.

Beyond the details of the story and how it came to be filmed, though, one of the most interesting questions about The Birds is why Hitchcock made it in the first place. It took its title from a short story by English author Daphne du Maurier, but beyond the basic idea of people being attacked by birds it didn't take much else from it. The storyline was pure Hitchcock. So where did it come from?

It turns out that his inspiration was a strange and alarming incident that happened just a few miles from his home in California. This book uncovers the truth behind the plot as well as other factoids that fascinate any fan of the film.

EXPOSING JACK THE STRIPPER: A BIOGRAPHY OF THE WORST SERIAL KILLER YOU'VE PROBABLY NEVER HEARD OF

Jack the Ripper may get all the fame, but his 1960s counterpart, Jack the Stripper, will really send shivers down your spine. At least six women, all prostitutes, were murdered at his hand--possibly more. Most intriguing of all...he was never caught.

The crimes, though often forgotten today, inspired the crime novel "Goodbye Piccadilly, Farewell Leicester Square," which Alfred Hitchcock turned into the 1972 movie, "Frenzy."

Go inside the hunt for this brutal killer in this gripping short biography.

THE PERFECT CRIME: THE REAL LIFE CRIME THAT INSPIRED HITCHCOCK'S ROPE

Leopold and Loeb were two wealthy law students who could buy anything. But they wanted the one thing that no amount of money could buy: life. They wanted to create the Perfect Crime--to kidnap and murder a 14-year-old boy for the thrill of getting away with murder.

The crime was so horrifying that even legendary filmmaker Alfred Hitchcock took notice and directed his version of the story: Rope. But the real story of the Rope is much more brutal and suspenseful than even Hitchcock could do justice to. Read the real history in this thrilling true crime book.

THE TRUE STORY BEHIND ALFRED HITCHCOCK'S THE WRONG MAN

The Wrong Man tells the incredible tale of an innocent man falsely accused of a crime. That in itself is hardly an unusual story, but in this case a string of unlikely coincidences and sheer bad luck built a seemingly airtight case against him. It seemed that the entire justice system was deaf to his pleas and all too willing to ignore the evidence his defenders had worked so hard to unearth. In the end it was only a slip by the real perpetrator that proved his innocence.

While the movie certainly had it's share of truth, it was still a movie, and parts were fabricated. This book tells the real story behind the movie.

NEWSLETTER OFFER

Don't forget to sign up for your newsletter to grab your free book:

http://www.absolutecrime.com/newsletter

NOTES

[1] Berkeley, *Charles de Gaulle*

http://web.archive.org/web/20060107012026/http://econ16
1.berkeley.edu/TCEH/charlesdegaulle.html
2 Reagan, G, Military Anecdotes, 1992, Guinness Publishing
3 Werth, A, De Gaulle, 1965
4 Crimetime.co.uk, Cathi Unsworth on Bad Penny Blues

http://www.crimetime.co.uk/community/mag.php/showcom
ments/1406

5 TruTV Crime Library, Jack The Stripper:A Scandalous Death?

http://www.trutv.com/library/crime/serial_killers/unsolved/ja
ck_the_stripper/3.html

6 Life Magazine, April 26, 1968, The French Spy Scandal
http://jfk.hood.edu/Collection/Weisberg%20Subject%20I
ndex%20Files/D%20Disk/deVosjoli%20Philippe%20Thyraud/I
tem%2001.pdf
7 CNN.com, Spies – Joe Bulik

http://www2.gwu.edu/~nsarchiv/coldwar/interviews/episode
-21/bulik1.html
8 Air Force Magazine, August 2005, Airpower and the Cuban Missile Crisis

http://www.airforcemag.com/MagazineArchive/Pages/2005/
August%202005/0805u2.aspx

9 Cold War International History Project Bulletin, R.
Malinovsky to N.S. Krushchev, 28 October 1962
http://alternatewars.com/WW3/Cuba/Anadyr_U-
2_Shootdown.htm

10 "Suvorov, Viktor," Inside the Soviet Army, Macmillan
Publishing, 1982

11 Life Magazine, April 26, 1968, The French Spy Scandal
http://jfk.hood.edu/Collection/Weisberg%20Subject%20I
ndex%20Files/D%20Disk/deVosjoli%20Philippe%20Thyraud

12 Fursenko, A and Naftali, T, Inside the Kremlin's Cold
War, 1996, Harvard Press

13 BBC Home, 1963: Moscow jails British 'spy'

http://news.bbc.co.uk/onthisday/hi/dates/stories/may/11/ne
wsid_2524000/2524239.stm

14 Life Magazine, April 26, 1968, The French Spy Scandal

15 Life Magazine, April 26, 1968, The French Spy Scandal

16 Turner Classic Movies, Topaz (1969)

http://www.tcm.com/tcmdb/title/93636/Topaz/articles.html

www.ingramcontent.com/pod-product-compliance
Lightning Source LLC
Chambersburg PA
CBHW051027030426
42336CB00015B/2754

9 781629 176406